AF126360

BOOK ANALYSIS

By Genevieve Zimantas

Go Tell It on the Mountain

by James Baldwin

JAMES BALDWIN

AMERICAN NOVELIST, PLAYWRIGHT, ESSAYIST, AND SHORT STORY WRITER

- **Born in New York City in 1924.**
- **Died in Saint-Paul-de-Vence, France in 1987.**
- **Notable works:**
  - *Notes of a Native Son* (1955), essays
  - *Giovanni's Room* (1956), novel
  - *The Fire Next Time* (1963), essays

Born in Harlem during the height of the Harlem Renaissance (New York cultural movement of the 1920s), James Baldwin led a crowded but lonely childhood. Abused by his stepfather for being a bastard, the result of a relationship his mother had before their marriage, and intelligent in a way that set him apart from his peers even at an early age, Baldwin grew up in relative poverty, often helping to take care of his eight younger siblings. Maturing into adolescence as a young black man in a world still plagued by violent and explicit racism, and gradually coming to understand that he was bisexual, Baldwin also struggled to find acceptance beyond the family home in the city where he had been born.

He chose to leave New York at the age of 24 and emigrated to France where, arriving first in Paris, he would produce much of the work for which he is most celebrated. Today recognised as one of the most important minds of the 20th century, Baldwin was an early proponent of black rights and gay rights in America. His work was also the subject of the critically acclaimed 2016 documentary, *I Am Not Your Negro*, directed by Raoul Peck.

GO TELL IT ON THE MOUNTAIN

SEMI-AUTOBIOGRAPHICAL TALE ABOUT COMING OF AGE IN 1930S HARLEM

- **Genre:** novel
- **Reference edition:** Baldwin, J. (1992) Go Tell It on the Mountain. In: T. Morrison, ed. *James Baldwin: Early Novels and Stories*. New York: The Library of America, pp. 1-216.
- **1st edition:** 1953
- **Themes:** racism, religion, family, sexuality, gender, class, belonging, justice, faith

Go Tell It on the Mountain tells the story of John Grimes' 14th birthday, from the time he wakes up that morning and finds his family in the kitchen, until the following morning when, after a night of religious and historical realisation, he arrives home again, uncertain and wary of his father, himself, and his future. Mirroring its author's own childhood experiences and family history,

Baldwin's first major work is a lyrical and narrative triumph. It evidences at once a startling fury at the circumstances of his characters' lives, especially the ingrained and systemic racism which constrains them, and an extraordinary sense of pathos.

Written in Paris, where Baldwin emigrated after leaving the United States, *Go Tell It on the Mountain* is still widely read, studied, and beloved as an important American classic. It was made into a film for television directed by Stan Lathan in 1984.

SUMMARY

PART I: TOUGH BEGINNINGS

John Grimes' story begins on his 14th birthday, when he awakes filled with shame because, the narrator tells us, "he remembered [...] that he had sinned" (p. 16) by touching himself. John falls back asleep before awaking again, some time later, and making his way to the family kitchen, convinced that his family will not have remembered his birthday.

In the kitchen, John introduces one of the major questions of the novel by asking his mother if his father—the man who is really his stepfather—is a good man. John's mother dismisses the question and asks John to do some housework before calling him back into the kitchen, where she gives him some money for his birthday and sends him off to use it. John goes to Central Park and then uses the money to buy a ticket to the movie houses where he sees a sensational historical film.

Returning home after the film, John finds his younger brother Roy on the couch and the rest of the family, including his aunt Florence, around him, trying to staunch the blood coming from Roy's forehead. Roy had been in a fight with a group of young white men. The incident and ensuing injury causes an argument in which Gabriel Grimes beats his wife and then Roy for interfering until his sister Florence comes between them and stares her brother down, shaming him for his mistreatment of his wife and son.

John goes to church where he helps the preacher's son Elisha to clean the floor of the altar. Later, his parents and his aunt arrive and join them for evening prayers.

PART II: FAMILY PRAYERS

The next section of the novel presents the early lives of John's parents and aunt in a series of 'prayers' or flashbacks:

Florence's prayer tells the story of how she left home in the South and moved North to make a life for herself, about how she fell in love with an irresponsible man named Frank, and about how he left her before going off to war was and being killed in France.

Gabriel's prayer tells the story of his early days as a preacher and of his first marriage to Deborah, whom he married even after she had been raped by a group of white men, partially to show that he was holy enough to redeem her. Gabriel cheats on Deborah, however, with a beautiful young woman named Esther who works in the same white-man's house as him during the day. Esther becomes pregnant and, because Gabriel refuses to recognise either her or her unborn child, her parents send her away to Chicago where she dies. Esther's son is raised by his grandparents and Gabriel watches him grown up from afar, but never recognises him as his own son. This first son, named Roy, eventually goes North himself to Chicago, where he dies in a bar fight. Gabriel and Deborah never have children and she eventually dies of ill health.

Elizabeth's prayer tells the story of her youth after her mother dies and her father leaves her in the care of an uncaring aunt. While living with her aunt, Elizabeth meets a young black man named Richard and the two fall madly in love.

They move together to New York and plan to get married, but Richard is accused of armed robbery and imprisoned. He is eventually acquitted, but the trauma of the false accusation and of the racial injustice of the world is too much for Richard and he kills himself without ever knowing that Elizabeth is pregnant, that John is on the way, or that he would have been a father.

PART III: LYRIC OF EMOTION AND EXPERIENCE

Following the 'prayers' of his family members, John falls into a kind of trance and passes the whole night of his 14th birthday on the floor of the church, surrounded by darkness and far away from the singing of the others in the room.

He awakes the next morning and the small evening congregation who stayed with him and kept vigil leave the church together to head for their respective homes. On the way home, Elisha promises to watch over John and to help guide him on his path towards God. In a very different conversation, Florence tells her brother about a letter Deborah had once sent her, proving that

Deborah knew all along about her husband's first illegitimate son. Florence threatens that she is going to see justice done, and Gabriel made to answer for his sins, before she dies.

The novel ends on an uncertain note of transition as John parts from Elisha and walks the distance to his house from the street, with his parents just behind him. Nothing decisive has happened to change John's family circumstances, and his optimism is tinged with wariness, but his old wounds have been exposed to fresh air and he feels himself to be "on my way" (p. 215) somewhere.

CHARACTER STUDY

JOHN GRIMES

John Grimes is the 14-year-old protagonist of Baldwin's novel. He is bright and the target of his father's most intense abuse. The result of his mother's tragic love affair with a man named Richard, who killed himself after being falsely accused of armed robbery, John is unaware of his real parentage and bewildered by his adoptive father's hatred.

ROY GRIMES

John's younger brother and the namesake of Gabriel's first illegitimate child, the Roy of John's present is a hot-blooded and angry young man who does not care at all about the Church. He gets injured in a fight between a group of his friends and a group of young white men towards the beginning of the novel and intervenes after his father begins hitting his mother, only to have his father turn that violent rage on him.

ELIZABETH GRIMES

Already the mother of four young children, John's mother is pregnant again at the beginning of the novel. Despite her difficult life, she is "dressed up on that day, and looked almost young" (p. 9) when John first enters the kitchen on his birthday. She wears "the close fitting white cap that was the uniform of holy women" (*ibid*.) and tries to protect her children from their father, all the while conscious of what her life, and John's life, would have been had Gabriel not decided to make them legitimate and protect them with his offer of marriage.

GABRIEL GRIMES

Gabriel Grimes is the patriarch of the family, a passionate, angry, and often violent figure looming over the rest of the household. Really John's stepfather, Gabriel does not hide his preference for Roy over John or make much effort to love his wife's first illegitimate son. Convinced that God "done forgive me a long time ago" (p. 206) for his past sins, Gabriel is a man who has had a difficult life but who also refuses to soften in order to make the lives of those around him any easier.

AUNT FLORENCE

Gabriel's sister and John's aunt, Florence is one of the strongest characters in the novel and the only one determined to stand up to her brother and end the cycle of his abuse: "I'm going to find some *way*," she says, to "tell *everybody*, about the blood the Lord's anointed is got on his hands" (p. 208). Still disappointed by the failure of her marriage and real love affair with Frank, and humiliated by her usurpation by the woman he lived with after he left her, Florence laments that she could not have protected her friend Elizabeth from an even worse fate with her brother and tries to protect Elizabeth and her children.

ELISHA

An older boy in the church and the preacher's son, Elisha is "already saved" (p. 11) at the beginning of the novel and likely the object of John's desire. Dedicated to the ways of the Church, Elisha rejects his relationship with Ella Mae, a female companion and fellow churchgoer, when her father publicly identifies the risks their relationship poses to their respective relationships with God. At the end of the novel, he represents an alternative source of family and community to John's own tumultuous home-life, as well as a possible outlet for John's same-sex desires.

DEBORAH

Gabriel's first wife, Deborah is a deeply tragic figure in Baldwin's novel. Gang raped by a group of white men when she is only 16, she becomes a kind of "holy fool" (p. 104), taking their sin as her own, and dedicates her life first to the Church and then to the Church as it manifests through Gabriel. Aware of Gabriel's infidelity throughout his affair and of his illegitimate child, Deborah nevertheless refuses to confront her husband. It is after she dies of ill health that he decides to move North like his sister.

FRANK

Florence's husband of ten years, Frank is benign but impractical, bad with money, and unfaithful. He leaves Florence when he realises that she no longer wants him around and starts up with another woman. He dies as a soldier in France during the First World War.

RICHARD

Richard is Elizabeth's first love and John's biological father. Determined to educate himself as much as any white man so that "no white son-of-a-bitch *nowhere* never talk *me* down, and make me feel like *I* was dirt" (p. 161), he brings Elizabeth to museums, plays, films, and parts of the city she had never known before. The narrator observes that he "never 'watched' his language with her" (p. 160) but that Elizabeth gradually came to take this as "evidence of his love" (*ibid.*) rather than of any "contempt because she had fallen so easily" (*ibid.*). After leaving her one evening, Richard is picked up with a group of other black men and accused alongside them of the robbery they had just committed. He is badly abused in prison and, even though he is eventually released and cleared of all charges, kills himself by slitting his wrists because of the cruelty and injustice he would never be able to unsee.

ESTHER

Esther is the young woman Gabriel takes as a mistress during his marriage to Deborah and "the mother of the first Royal" (p. 110). Described as a "thin, vivid, dark-eyes girl" (p. 111), Esther comes from what Gabriel considers "sinful people" (*ibid.*) and elicits both his "pity" (*ibid.*) and his disdain. She dies of unspecified causes while up North giving birth to their son.

ROY (ESTHER AND GABRIEL'S SON)

The first Roy in Gabriel's life is the illegitimate son he conceives with Esther during their extramarital affair. She goes to Chicago and names him Royal, because Gabriel had once told her that would be the name of his first child, "a royal child" (p. 134), because "the line of the faithful was a holy line" (*ibid.*). Gabriel never claims his first son and so Roy never knows that Gabriel is his father. He dies in a bar fight up 'North' while still a young man.

ANALYSIS

SOUTH AND NORTH

The idea that there are more opportunities for black people in the Northern states than in the South is an important promise for the characters of *Go Tell It on the Mountain*. Almost all of the characters of Elizabeth and Gabriel's generation make the move North, as did "some 500 000 black southerners during the war years" (Williams, 2010: 4), reflecting, as Chad Williams argues, "their desires for social, political, and economic equality" (*ibid*.). Indeed, the move North does afford Baldwin's characters certain rights or opportunities not available to them in the South. For Florence, the move North repre-sents freedom from her mother and brother, while for Elizabeth and Richard it means the opportunity to work and start a life together. For all of them it means a distance from the kind of violence to which Deborah and the young lynching victim are subjected early in the novel's historical narrative.

But the realities of racism are not wholly limited to the South in either Baldwin's novel or in American history, a fact of which all of his characters are inevitably made aware: Esther dies alone in Chicago, as does her son when he returns to the city years later and he gets into a fight in a bar there; Frank goes to war, as "nearly 400 000 African American soldiers did" (Williams, 2010: 3) and dies; and Richard, perhaps the clearest example of the illusory nature of 'justice' in America's North, is falsely accused of armed robbery and imprisoned awaiting trial for a crime he did not commit.

America's North affords Baldwin's characters an important degree of mobility and anonymity; after Richard is arrested, Elizabeth goes into one of the "downtown establishments, where only white people were" (p. 167), almost looking for someone to attack her: "But no one touched her; no one spoke" (*ibid.*). Their indifference to her presence is different from the hatred Gabriel feels walking down a street in the South, surrounded by white men "itching to kill" (p. 136), but it is not freedom or safety. The North of the country is still, for Baldwin's characters, a white space in which they are identified, first and foremost, by their blackness.

THE PLACE OF THE CHURCH

The Church and the Bible play a prominent role in Baldwin's novel and in its protagonist's young life. The church the family attend, we learn, is "not very far away," just "four blocks up Lennox Avenue" (p. 9) and the Grimes family spends every Sunday morning there. Excerpts from the Bible and references to its stories appear throughout Baldwin's text, interwoven with his own language, and his characters actively read and reference the book themselves. *Go Tell It on the Mountain* also has an ambivalent relationship with the Church, however, as an institution which rewards men like Gabriel with social capital as deacons while allowing them to beat their families into piety at home.

The ambivalent but persistent relationship all of Baldwin's characters have with the Church, whether by choice or against their will, frustrates characters like Roy, who berates his mother for her insistent support: "You think that's all that's in the world is jails and churches?" (p. 23) he asks her. For Elizabeth, the dichotomy is almost a true one, her life suspended between Richard, who did not care what anyone thought and wrongfully ended up in prison, and Gabriel, who uses his relationship with the Church to justify his abuse of her but who is also there to feed and protect her and her children from the cruelties of the world beyond their family home.

The Church, in Baldwin's novel, is therefore at once a hypocritical institution and a necessary cornerstone of the black community in which John lives—one which keeps young black men out of prison and out of trouble, but also one which perpetuates their worst habits.

All of this complexity and ambivalence bleeds into John's relationship with the Church as he lies on the 'threshing-floor'. He resigns himself to a world filled with the "many faces" of "the Devil" (p. 212) like his own stepfather, who does not smile back when John tries to connect with him, or anyone else who hurts the people around him, the people with whom he shares the world.

BLACK WOMEN, SUFFERING

Many of the most sympathetic and long-suffering characters in *Go Tell It on the Mountain* are female: Esther, Florence, Elizabeth, and Deborah all suffer terribly and, unlike Gabriel or either Roy (Esther's son Roy or Elizabeth's son Roy), are not themselves responsible for any acts of suffering or violence. They are all, as Florence observes to herself during her marriage to Frank, "given the same cruel destiny, born to suffer the weight of men" (p. 78).

The trials and tribulations Baldwin's female characters face are similar to those of white female characters in other novels written about the same period: Frank drinks away most of his earnings before Florence can use them for groceries in the same way that the mining men in D. H. Lawrence's (English novelist, 1885-1930) *Sons and Lovers* (1913) do. But, as is true of Baldwin's narrative universe as a whole, these women also face additional prejudice because of their race, and have recourse to fewer alternative sources of aid than their white counterparts. Indeed, after Richard is arrested the most immediate threat to Elizabeth becomes the police officers who inform her of his fate.

Despite the fact that his portrayals of these characters are largely sympathetic, Baldwin's depiction of women has come under criticism for being more flat and less nuanced than his depictions of men. As Trudier Harris argues, "most of the women believe themselves to be guilty of some crime or condition of existence that demands their doing penance" (Harris, 1985: 5) and which comes to define them in a way that John's shame at having masturbated to thoughts of Elisha do not come to define him despite his similar sense of guilt and shame.

This distinction between Baldwin's treatment of the male and female characters in his novel does not necessarily indicate that Baldwin himself saw them in more simplistic terms. As Harris concedes, Baldwin shows his female characters' "limitations [to] spring from two sources" (Harris, 1985: 12): other, older women in their lives and the Church. And yet, while Baldwin's fictions make room within their representations of masculinity to explore same-sex desire, "lesbianism as a concept does not surface in his books" (Harris, 1985: 8).

All of Baldwin's female characters suffer. Tragically, just as the holy men in Deborah's village define her by her childhood trauma, Baldwin allows them to be defined by that suffering.

FURTHER REFLECTION

SOME QUESTIONS TO THINK ABOUT...

- The plot of this novel is not overly complex. What does it use to drive its narrative instead?
- Is it significant that the only time John leaves Harlem is after his mother has given him some money for his birthday? What does this suggest about the relationship between money and mobility?
- Why does Baldwin describe the drops of Roy's blood on the floor and stairs leading up to the apartment as "smudged coins of blood" (p. 39)?
- What is the significance of dirt and 'grime' in this novel? What instances of dirtiness can you find? What do they mean?
- What is the "bleaching cream" (p. 84) Deborah applies during her prayer? What is the purpose of this cream? How does Baldwin's narrator think about it?
- What is the source of *Go Tell It on the Mountain*'s title? What role does music play in John's

spiritual journey? In the lives of Baldwin's characters more generally?

- Where do you think John is 'on his way' to at the end of the novel?
- How does Baldwin's quotation of the Bible throughout his novel impact its message? Does the integration of these passages make his book more or less religious? What effect do the italicised passages have on the way the text looks?

We want to hear from you!
Leave a comment on your online library
and share your favourite books on social media!

FURTHER READING

REFERENCE EDITION

- Baldwin, J. (1992) Go Tell It on the Mountain. In: T. Morrison, ed. *James Baldwin: Early Novels and Stories*. New York: The Library of America, pp. 1-216.

REFERENCE STUDIES

- Harris, T. (1985) *Black Women in the Fiction of James Baldwin*. Knoxville: University of Tennessee Press.

- Lawrence, D. H. (2002) *Sons and Lovers*. New York: Dover Publications, Inc.

- Williams, C. (2010) *Torchbearers of Democracy: African American Soldiers in the World War I Era*. Chapel Hill: The University of North Carolina Press.

ADDITIONAL SOURCES

- Baldwin, J. (2017) *Notes of a Native Son*. London: Penguin Classics.

- Keith, C. (2004) *Black Manhood in James Baldwin, Ernest J. Gaines, and August Wilson*. Chicago: University of Illinois Press.

ADAPTATIONS

- *Go Tell It on the Mountain*. (1984) [Film]. Stan Lathan. Dir. USA: PBS.

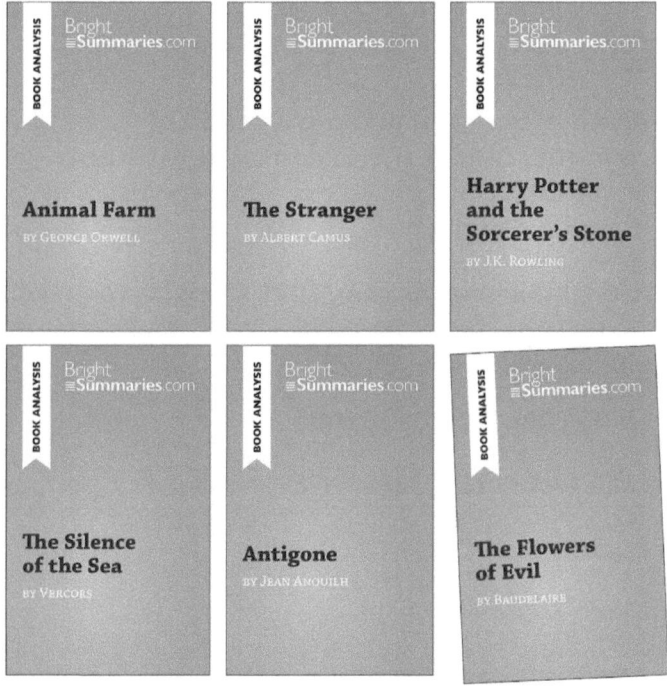

www.brightsummaries.com

Ebook EAN: 9782808017886

Paperback EAN: 9782808017893

Legal Deposit: D/2019/12603/61

Cover: © Primento

Digital conception by Primento, the digital partner of
publishers.